# The COLORS
## of
## Christmas

## A Devotional Prayer Journal

### BARBOUR BOOKS
An Imprint of Barbour Publishing, Inc.

© 2018 by Barbour Publishing, Inc.

ISBN 978-1-68322-712-0

Devotions by Dena Dyer.

Journal prompts created by Linda Hang.

Scripture quotations are taken from the King James Version of the Bible.

Published by Barbour Books, an imprint of Barbour Publishing, Inc., 1810 Barbour Drive, Uhrichsville, Ohio 44683, www.barbourbooks.com

*Our mission is to inspire the world with the life-changing message of the Bible.*

Member of the
Evangelical Christian
Publishers Association

Printed in China.

*Experience the Colors of Christmas
with this inspiring prayer journal.*

This uniquely creative Christmas prayer journal
features four topics—each assigned to a festive color
of the holiday season. Quickly and easily locate a topic
that appeals to you, then read faith-building devotionals
and begin to journal your very own thoughts and
prayers. Encouraging scripture selections and
journaling prompts will continue to inspire
you with every turn of the page.

---

Your Guide to the
Colors of Christmas

Love—RED

Joy—GOLD

Peace—WHITE

Hope—GREEN

# Love
## One of the Greatest Gifts

*In the multitude of my thoughts*
*within me thy comforts delight my soul.*
PSALM 94:19

When the angels spoke to the shepherds, they declared: "Glory to God in the highest, and on earth peace, good will toward men." (Luke 2:14).

Why did they say *this*? Maybe they knew that when we think about God, we are often ashamed of our weaknesses, trapped by our insecurities, and deathly afraid we'll never be accepted. Perhaps the angels were reassuring the shepherds—lower-class, smelly laborers—that it was okay to approach *this* Messiah. . .because they had already pleased God.

Can you accept the truth that He loves you beyond what you can ever imagine? Can you rest in His approval and place your identity squarely on His shoulders, not on your appearance or accomplishments? If you can, it will change your life.

When you feel comforted by such a glorious truth, you can then comfort others. When you know—all the way to the tips of your toes—that He delights in you, it changes the way you think, believe, and act.

We are beloved. It's one of the greatest gifts of that first Christmas.

*God is love; and he that dwelleth in love dwelleth in God, and God in him.*

1 JOHN 4:16

No Person or entity can come between me and God's Love for me. Satan tries to distract inter- rupt, -fere, CONfuse, Attack when we are tired, Revive up our spirit in rest, relax, hydrate nutrient music, art, sewing, puzzling, painting, making, healing running, playing, praying, watching, waiting.

*That ye, being rooted and grounded in love, may be able to comprehend with all saints what is the breadth, and length, and depth,  and height; and to know the love of Christ, which passeth knowledge,  that ye might be filled with all the fulness of God.*

EPHESIANS 3:17–19

FEAR        I must put on Jesus
a          fill my self w/ his Love
l          H.s.  sheild of faith,
s          belt of truth
e          Helmet of salvation
          Sword of

          Know that I CAN Do
All  things th___ Christ.

*And this I pray, that your love*
*may abound yet more and more. . .*
PHILIPPIANS **1:9**

WHERE HAS GOD PLACED YOU TO SHINE HIS LOVE?

# Drawing Others to Jesus

*The people that walked in darkness have seen a great light:*
*they that dwell in the land of the shadow of death,*
*upon them hath the light shined.*

ISAIAH 9:2

---

"Good King Wenceslas looked out on the Feast of Stephen/When the snow lay round about, deep and crisp and even. . .You who will bless the poor shall yourselves find blessing."

Do you know the story behind the Christmas carol "Good King Wenceslas"? In the mid-1800s, prolific Anglican minister and musician John Neale wrote the words, and set them to an old Swedish tune, to honor a Bohemian Duke named Wenceslas for his charitable works.

After Wenceslas' father died, the eighteen-year-old took over governing what is now the Czech Republic. He reformed the judicial system, encouraged people of faith to build congregations, and showed Christian concern for those in poverty. He was known to chop firewood for orphans and widows. He would even carry the heavy load on his own shoulders in the snow.

As Christ-followers, we are on a mission in the world. Just as the star over Bethlehem shone to help the three magi find the baby Jesus, we have been placed in our cities and jobs at this moment and for a specific purpose. The joy and peace He gives us, especially in the midst of difficulties, shine brightly into a world groaning with despair.

Wenceslas knew it was a disciple's duty to seek justice, minister to the poor, and carry others' burdens. When we do, people around us will be drawn to Jesus.

Dec. 24, 2019

Eve bit the apples. Jesus was tempted; but, He never sinned. Satan wants something. He wants our souls. He wants to take Jesus from the throne of Heaven. He wants to destroy every good thing. He wants chaos, division and separation among people, friends, family, church and community.

America is a great country without indoctrinating all the ways of the world that have proven NOT to work.

We need Light. The Light of the Savior. We need Love. To Love And to be Loved. We need the Stripes. The Stripes of our Savior. You must receive the Stripes (blood) of the Savior as our only Hope. Jesus is our Hope for everything GOOD GOD wants for us, his Children. GOD wants you to call on Him for everything. He wants to be a part of everything we think about and want to do & become. Take yourself to the Cross of Jesus & surrender All.

*Be kindly affectioned one to another with brotherly love.*

ROMANS 12:10

IS IT EASIER OR MORE DIFFICULT TO LOVE OTHERS
DURING THE HOLIDAYS? WHY?

*And walk in love, as Christ also hath loved us, and hath given himself for us an offering and a sacrifice to God for a sweetsmelling savour.*

EPHESIANS 5:2

# HOW IS GOD LEADING YOU TO BE
# GENEROUS THIS CHRISTMAS SEASON?

*Jesus said unto him, Thou shalt love the Lord thy God
with all thy heart, and with all thy soul, and with all thy mind.
This is the first and great commandment. And the second is
like unto it, Thou shalt love thy neighbour as thyself.*

MATTHEW 22:37–39

REFLECT ON THE TWO GREATEST COMMANDMENTS—
TO LOVE GOD AND OTHERS.

*For God so loved the world, that he gave his only begotten Son, that whosoever believeth in him should not perish, but have everlasting life.*

JOHN 3:16

WHY IS CHRISTMAS THE PERFECT TIME TO SHARE GOD'S LOVE?

*Keep yourselves in the love of God.*

JUDE 1:21

# HOW CAN YOU STAY FOCUSED ON LOVE IN A
## STRESSFUL AND HECTIC TIME OF YEAR?

# Season of Praise

*He is thy praise, and he is thy God, that hath done for thee these
great and terrible things, which thine eyes have seen.*

DEUTERONOMY 10:21

Anna was the New Testament's only named prophetess. Luke describes her as a widow—only married seven years before losing her husband—and a fixture at the temple. Anna worshipped day and night, fasting and praying. For decades after her husband's death had left her alone, Anna hadn't grieved without hope or relied on the charity of others to keep her going. Instead, she clung tight to God, serving Him at the temple.

When Mary and Joseph came with the baby Jesus to His purification ceremony, Anna—along with Simeon, a priest—realized that she was beholding the Messiah. How did she know? The years spent in God's holy presence had given her an intimacy with Him. She heard His voice and knew His truth.

In fact, after she saw the baby Jesus, she began to speak about the child to all who were looking for the redemption of Jerusalem (Luke 2:38). Anna became one of the first Christian missionaries!

God longs for us to spend time at the feet of Jesus, worshipping. We need this time (especially during the hectic weeks leading up to and during the holidays) to correct our perspective and reorder our priorities. Without worship and praise, our minds become polluted by the world, and we simply cannot make godly decisions. However, when we know His voice, we can obey Him and share His love with those around us.

Make time this season to worship your King. You won't regret it.

WHAT DOES SPENDING TIME AT JESUS' FEET LOOK LIKE IN YOUR LIFE?

*I will love thee, O LORD, my strength.*

**PSALM 18:1**

# How can you grow your love of Jesus during the holidays?

*Let all your things be done with charity.*

1 Corinthians 16:14

# WHAT DO YOU LOVE ABOUT CHRISTMAS?

*He that loveth his brother abideth in the light,*
*and there is none occasion of stumbling in him.*

1 JOHN 2:10

# HOW HAS LOVING OTHERS BEEN A BLESSING IN YOUR LIFE?

*We love him, because he first loved us.*

1 John 4:19

How is God's great love for the world a model for our love—
at Christmastime and throughout the year?

> *And now abideth faith, hope, charity,*
> *these three; but the greatest of these is charity.*
>
> 1 CORINTHIANS 13:13

Charity has to be given away.

# WHY IS LOVE SO POWERFUL?

Love is the living FORCE of Power

# Abundant Love

*That they do good, that they be rich in good works,*
*ready to distribute, willing to communicate. . .*

1 Timothy 6:18

---

In the film version of *Little Women* starring Winona Ryder, the poor-but-happy March sisters Jo, Amy, and Meg sit down to a Christmas breakfast of delicacies reserved for holidays. However, after hearing from their sister Beth that a neighbor woman has children with nothing to eat, they decide to share the little they have with the family in need. Their mother ("Marmie") has taught them from infancy the biblical virtue of sacrifice.

In stark contrast, in the play *A Christmas Carol*, Ebeneezer Scrooge hates Christmas and makes everyone around him miserable with his complaints and selfishness. He loves money more than people, can't stand the thought of generosity, and loathes closing the office, even if just one day a year.

Over the course of one eventful night, Scrooge is taught what really matters, and he changes his ways. He learns to see others through more compassionate eyes and forgives himself for his horrid past.

Our sinful hearts often veer between the two extremes: Beth, who knew wealth is more than riches and was willing to share what little she had with someone in need, and Scrooge, who held tightly to his money because he was insecure and greedy. This Christmas, let's resolve to hold loosely to the earthly treasures God has gifted us with and share freely.

When we share, we model the abundant love He has shown us in Jesus' birth, death, and resurrection. In doing so, we draw others closer to the Light that overcame—and is still overcoming—the world's darkness.

## In what ways are you a Beth or a Scrooge when it comes to giving?

*Let love be without dissimulation.*
*Abhor that which is evil; cleave to that which is good.*

ROMANS 12:9

ARE PEOPLE MORE OR LESS LOVING AROUND CHRISTMAS? WHY?

*Owe no man any thing, but to love one another:*
*for he that loveth another hath fulfilled the law.*

ROMANS 13:8

# BEYOND THE GIFTS, WHAT SAYS LOVE THE MOST AT CHRISTMAS?

But I say unto you, Love your enemies, bless them
that curse you, do good to them that hate you, and pray
for them which despitefully use you, and persecute you.

MATTHEW 5:44

## HOW CAN YOU "LOVE YOUR ENEMIES" THIS CHRISTMAS?

*Though I speak with the tongues of men and of angels, and have not charity, I am become as sounding brass, or a tinkling cymbal.*

1 CORINTHIANS 13:1

# To whom can you reach out in love this holiday season?

# HOW CAN YOU KEEP A LOVING SPIRIT ALL YEAR LONG?

*Father, thank You for Your provision. Help me not to worry, but instead be consistently aware of all the ways You take care of me and my family. I know You are faithful to provide all that I need. Forgive me for doubting You and—too often—taking matters into my own hands. Your ways are better, Lord. Help me to live a life of love and abound in thanksgiving. Amen.*

# Joy

## Shout "Hallelujah!"

*The LORD thy God in the midst of thee is mighty;*
*he will save, he will rejoice over thee with joy; he will*
*rest in his love, he will joy over thee with singing.*

ZEPHANIAH 3:17

Did you know there are over 200 verses in the Bible containing the word "rejoice"? Some passages urge us to rejoice over God's works and His gifts; others command us to rejoice always, even in hard times.

Rejoicing is a habit which draws us closer to the heart of God and keeps us in tune with His purposes. Like prayer, it's also a powerful weapon against Satan's schemes. In 2 Chronicles 20 (KJV), the Israelites were facing enormous odds against three enemy armies. However, God told the Israelites through the musician and prophet Jahaziel to "stand ye still" and see what God would do. The next morning, Jehosophat appointed "singers unto the LORD" to go in front of the army and praise their Creator. While they rejoiced in the Lord, the Israelites' foes destroyed one another.

What a perfect picture of the power of praise! Rejoicing in God during turbulent times—those moments when hope seems like a distant memory and despair threatens to drown us—tells the devil that we won't be defeated by mere circumstance. Instead, we trust in God's character and His promises, no matter what.

One way we can develop a habit of rejoicing is to remember that regardless of what we do or don't do, our Heavenly Father delights in us and will never leave us. With His love, He calms our fears. And—get this—He sings and *rejoices over us.*

Doesn't that make you want to shout "Hallelujah!"?

*As the bridegroom rejoiceth over the bride,*
*so shall thy God rejoice over thee.*

ISAIAH 62:5

**WHAT THOUGHTS COME TO MIND WHEN
YOU THINK OF GOD REJOICING OVER YOU?**

What causes you to rejoice this Christmas?

*I will praise thee, O Lord my God, with all my heart:*
*and I will glorify thy name for evermore.*

PSALM 86:12

*And my soul shall be joyful in the Lord:*
*it shall rejoice in his salvation.*

PSALM 35:9

## HOW CAN YOU CHOOSE JOY THIS CHRISTMAS?

WHY DO YOU THINK GOD WANTS US TO BE JOYFUL?

# Shared Abundance

*And thou shalt not glean thy vineyard, neither shalt thou
gather every grape of thy vineyard; thou shalt leave them
for the poor and stranger: I am the LORD your God.*

LEVITICUS 19:10

---

One summer, Barbara's father told her mother to "get out or else." She says
because God—and their mother—took care of them, she and her siblings never
felt poor. They gathered their courage, worked hard, and did whatever they
needed to in order to survive. However, when the holidays came, the family
knew that presents, clothes, and food would be sparse.

"One afternoon, I walked home from school and discovered a large
box on our front porch. . . . After we all got home, Mother opened it. Inside
were nice clothes for my sister and me. . .we tried on the beautiful clothes
and were happily outfitted for parties and church. We felt truly grateful for
being remembered."

Also, she says, "The first holiday in Baton Rouge, each elementary class
gathered canned goods for needy families. When my ten-year-old brother's
teacher asked if anyone in his class knew of someone who needed help,
he told her we did. In our previous town, we had helped deliver boxes of
food to needy families for years. Now it became our turn to graciously accept
one. At that time in our lives, it was truly a gift we needed."

What have you received from the Lord? Food, shelter, job, clothes? Why
not share your abundance with others this season? You might be the very
person who brings hope and joy to an otherwise hopeless situation. Who
knows? You might be the recipient of such kindness one day.

WHEN HAVE YOU SEEN EVEN A SMALL GIFT BRING JOY TO SOMEONE?

*I have shewed you all things, how that so labouring ye ought to support the weak, and to remember the words of the Lord Jesus, how he said, It is more blessed to give than to receive.*

ACTS 20:35

IS THERE REALLY MORE JOY IN GIVING THAN RECEIVING? WHY?

*I will greatly rejoice in the L*ORD*, my soul shall be joyful in my God;
for he hath clothed me with the garments of salvation, he hath covered
me with the robe of righteousness, as a bridegroom decketh himself
with ornaments, and as a bride adorneth herself with her jewels.*

ISAIAH **61:10**

WHAT HAS GOD DONE IN YOUR LIFE
OR GIVEN YOU THAT BRINGS YOU JOY?

*With trumpets and sound of cornet make*
*a joyful noise before the LORD, the King.*

PSALM 98:6

# HOW CAN YOU SPREAD JOY TODAY?

*Let the floods clap their hands:*
*let the hills be joyful together.*

**PSALM 98:8**

IS JOY, LIKE LAUGHTER, CONTAGIOUS? WHY?

*When they saw the star, they rejoiced with exceeding great joy.*

MATTHEW 2:10

HOW CAN YOU PROCLAIM "JOY TO THE WORLD" THIS CHRISTMAS?

# Inspired!

*Give unto the* LORD, *O ye kindreds of the people,*
*give unto the* LORD *glory and strength.*

PSALM 96:7

---

What inspires you about the Christmas season? For Darlene, it's "the simple beauty found in nature. God's attention to detail is astonishing!"

Cassandra says the "smells" of Christmas (gingerbread, pine, etc.) inspire her.

Dan, a music minister, is inspired by "the music and words of worship. They serve as tools to unify us under the banner of God's love, faithfulness, blessing, guidance, and mission."

Maybe it's a person who inspires you. Jill relates, "All the widows or widowers that I get to see over the Christmas season inspire me. This is a difficult time of year, but they are still smiling and laughing! They have no idea how much this encourages me to be thankful for my spouse and for each day God gives me."

Emily explains, "I'm inspired by the strength of our elders. My ninety-six-year-old grandmother is the hardest working lady I know. She inspires me to work harder. My father-in-law tells amazing stories of his childhood. It's a miracle many times over that he's alive today at the age of 99. Getting to be around them at this time of year is such a blessing. I appreciate each holiday I get to spend with them, more and more as the years pass. I haven't heard nearly enough of their stories yet!"

Let's pray that we would be an inspiration to others. We have the Answer to the world's problems, and Christmas is the perfect time to share it in winsome ways.

## WHAT INSPIRES YOU ABOUT THE CHRISTMAS SEASON?

*And Mary said, My soul doth magnify the Lord,*
*and my spirit hath rejoiced in God my Saviour.*

LUKE 1:46–47

**IF YOU ARE STRUGGLING TO FIND JOY THIS SEASON,
HOW CAN MARY'S FIRST CHRISTMAS INSPIRE YOU?**

*O come, let us sing unto the Lord: let us make*
*a joyful noise to the rock of our salvation.*

PSALM 95:1

# WHAT SPECIAL MEMORIES DO YOU HAVE OF REJOICING WITH FELLOW BELIEVERS AT CHRISTMAS?

*Thou wilt shew me the path of life: in thy presence is fulness of joy; at thy right hand there are pleasures for evermore.*

PSALM 16:11

WHAT GETS IN THE WAY OF JOY AT CHRISTMASTIME?
HOW CAN YOU GET AROUND THOSE OBSTACLES?

*Make a joyful noise unto the Lord, all the earth:*
*make a loud noise, and rejoice, and sing praise.*

PSALM 98:4

## WHAT HOLIDAY SONGS BOOST YOUR JOY?

*Let your light so shine before men, that they may see your good works, and glorify your Father which is in heaven.*

MATTHEW 5:16

# Celebrate!

*I am come that they might have life,
and that they might have it more abundantly.*

JOHN 10:10

---

Did the angels throw a party when Jesus was born? Did they celebrate when He returned to heaven after His death, resurrection, and ascension? I'm sure the heavens missed Him when He went to Earth.

The symbols of Christmas point to a future party we'll participate in, all because Jesus stepped off His celestial throne and clothed Himself with human flesh. The tree with its glittering ornaments represents eternal life; presents symbolize spiritual gifts of peace, joy, and love; the meal we share on Christmas Day foreshadows a breathtaking feast which all believers will enjoy.

Soon, our Savior and Bridegroom will return in power and might. He will destroy evil and bring justice on the earth. He will establish a Kingdom that will never end, where there will be no more war, racism, genocide, poverty, or despair.

Scripture doesn't give every detail about how or when Jesus' second coming will occur, but we know the answer to the most important question: *Who?* The eternal King will reign in glory, and every knee will bow to Him. We will finally, finally, be with our Bridegroom.

What began in Bethlehem will end in the New Jerusalem, and we will be there. We will sit at the table with Him, hardly able to contain our joy. It will be consummation of all our deepest hopes and dreams.

This picture stirs our hearts and quickens our spirit. We long for that day with groans that words can't express.

*Come quickly, Lord Jesus. Amen.*

# HOW DO YOU REJOICE?

*And the angel said unto them, Fear not: for, behold, I bring you good tidings of great joy, which shall be to all people.*

LUKE 2:10

## HOW DO YOU IMAGINE THE SHEPHERDS
### FELT AS THEY HEARD THE GOOD NEWS?

# HOW IS GOD OUR ULTIMATE SOURCE OF JOY?

*And now come I to thee; and these things I speak in the world,*
*that they might have my joy fulfilled in themselves.*

# WHY IS IT SO EASY TO EQUATE POSSESSIONS WITH JOY, WHEN WE SHOULD FIND JOY IN THE SPIRITUAL THINGS?

*Rejoice ye in that day, and leap for joy:*
*for, behold, your reward is great in heaven.*

LUKE 6:23

CONSIDER: OUR JOY IN HEAVEN WILL BE
INFINITELY GREATER THAN ANY JOY ON EARTH.

*I will sing of the mercies of the L*ORD *for ever: with my mouth will I make known thy faithfulness to all generations.*

PSALM 89:1

# How can you pass on a tradition of joy-filled holidays?

*God of angel armies, You are mighty to save. You are the same yesterday, today, and forever. I rejoice in Your works and ways. I praise You not only for who You are, but for what You do. When I am in need, You do battle for me. I don't have to fear because You are my deliverer. I don't need to worry because You are taking care of me. Thank You for living in me. Thank You for delighting in and rejoicing over me. You sing over me. . .I can hardly fathom that thought! You are so good to me! Amen.*

# SECTION 3

# Peace

## The Importance of Prayer

*Then hear thou in heaven their prayer and
their supplication, and maintain their cause.*

1 Kings 8:45

---

The weeks leading up to Christmas are often hectic. School programs, church activities, and preparation for holiday gatherings take a lot of energy and time. But let's not neglect moments of quiet prayer during Christmas though. Prayer is too important of a spiritual discipline to let it slide.

Have you ever heard someone say, "All we can do is pray"? Why do we think that prayer is the least important of all the acts of service we can give to someone in crisis? A meal can feed a friend's physical hunger, but prayer—and the peace that we impart when we lift someone up to the Father—feeds a spiritual need.

Also, we can pray any time of the day or night in any place we find ourselves. Prayer is a powerful tool against discouragement and, besides the Word of God, it is the main weapon we have to fight off the enemy of our souls. Intercessory prayer is a way to minister to those who might never hear our witness or accept our testimony. James 5:16 (KJV) says, "The effectual fervent prayer of a righteous man availeth much."

Ask God for the desire and discipline to pray for your immediate, extended, and church families. Use scriptures—especially those in Paul's letters—to personalize prayers for friends who need encouragement, faith, and endurance. Pray for missionaries and pastors in your circles, and don't forget to intercede for local, state, and national government officials.

*Pray unto the L*ORD *for it: for in the peace thereof shall ye have peace.*

JEREMIAH 29:7

## HOW DO PRAYER AND PEACE GO HAND IN HAND?

.......................................................................................................

.......................................................................................................

.......................................................................................................

.......................................................................................................

.......................................................................................................

.......................................................................................................

.......................................................................................................

.......................................................................................................

.......................................................................................................

.......................................................................................................

.......................................................................................................

.......................................................................................................

.......................................................................................................

.......................................................................................................

.......................................................................................................

.......................................................................................................

.......................................................................................................

.......................................................................................................

.......................................................................................................

.......................................................................................................

.......................................................................................................

.......................................................................................................

.......................................................................................................

.......................................................................................................

.......................................................................................................

.......................................................................................................

.......................................................................................................

*For unto us a child is born, unto us a son is given:*
*and the government shall be upon his shoulder:*
*and his name shall be called Wonderful, Counsellor,*
*The mighty God, The everlasting Father, The Prince of Peace.*

ISAIAH 9:6

## HOW DOES KNOWING THE PRINCE OF PEACE CHANGE HOW YOU LIVE (NOT ONLY DURING THE HOLIDAYS, BUT ALSO THE REST OF THE YEAR)?

*Grace be unto you, and peace, from God*
*our Father, and from the Lord Jesus Christ.*

**1 Corinthians 1:3**

## Is peace on your holiday wish list?

*The LORD will give strength unto his people;*
*the LORD will bless his people with peace.*

**PSALM 29:11**

# Do you need to rely more on God to fill you with peace? Why?

*LORD, thou wilt ordain peace for us:*
*for thou also hast wrought all our works in us.*

**ISAIAH 26:12**

## WHAT PRAYERS FOR PEACE ARE HEAVY ON YOUR HEART?

# Perfect Peace

*This is the rest wherewith ye may cause the weary to rest;*
*and this is the refreshing: yet they would not hear.*

ISAIAH **28:12**

---

At times, our desire to have a Pinterest-worthy Christmas overwhelms us, and we fill our calendars with nonessential activities. We get caught up in advertising hype, spend (and eat) more than we should, and experience post-holiday regret. Holiday gatherings with family turn into tense arenas of dysfunction. Idealism fades, reality sets in—and it isn't always pretty.

Why not try something different this year? Put "rest" on your to-do list. In 2 Thessalonians 1:7 (KJV), Paul the apostle wrote, "And to you who are troubled, rest with us." He was writing to the church at Thessalonica, a place which had undergone extreme persecution for a long period of time.

The word *rest* in this verse comes from the Greek word *anesis*. One scholar has said that the word was used in the secular Greek world to denote the release of a bowstring that has been under great pressure.

When we are under financial, job, or relational stress, God knows that we need times of reprieve. Not only does He give us permission to rest, He gives supernatural joy when we leave our concerns in His hands.

Prune your to-do list and social calendar. Ask your family what their favorite Christmas traditions are, and shelve the rest. After all, Jesus came so that we would have abundant life. His birth doesn't give us an excuse to be frenzied.

Loosen the bow and release your expectations. The result just might be joy—and perfect peace.

# How would you describe the holidays— peaceful or pressure-filled?

*Let us therefore follow after the things which make for peace.*

ROMANS 14:19

## IN WHAT WAYS COULD YOU MAKE REST BECOME A HOLIDAY TRADITION?

*To be spiritually minded is life and peace.*

**ROMANS 8:6**

## WHAT IS ONE THING YOU CAN FORGO THIS CHRISTMAS TO CREATE SPACE FOR PEACE?

*Seek peace, and pursue it.*

**Psalm 34:14**

# HOW CAN YOU CULTIVATE PEACE EVERY DAY OF THE YEAR?

*Glory to God in the highest, and on earth peace, good will toward men.*

**LUKE 2:14**

# What do the words of "Silent Night" say to you about peace?

*For he is our peace. . .*

EPHESIANS 2:14

**WHAT WOULD IT LOOK LIKE IF WE ALL CHOSE
GOD OVER THE BUSYNESS OF THE HOLIDAYS?**

# The Gift of Simple Pleasures

*Blessed are the meek: for they shall inherit the earth.*

MATTHEW 5:5

---

In 2003, newly-single Mark had a job, but it barely paid his bills. That year, he made stocking-stuffer gifts for his three kids, spent his small Christmas bonus on one large present for each child, and sent his close relatives long, handwritten letters. He turned down most of the social invitations he received to save money, time, and gas. At first, he felt sad about the necessary changes he'd made.

However, something happened as the December days slowly passed: He and the kids rediscovered the simple pleasures of the season. They baked cookies while listening to Christmas music. Mark unpacked once-forgotten books and movies, and the family spent many hours cuddled together on the couch. "I like this Christmas," his seven-year-old, Thomas, said one night.

"Me too," Mark replied.

Friends, are we complaining because God has us in a place we don't like? Are we praying for contentment in the midst of difficulty? Or are we begging God to change our circumstances?

Instead of groaning and fretting, let's say "no" to senseless busyness and carve out time to ponder the Lord's works and ways. When we look into His face, He fills us with wonder, gratitude, and peace. We can then pass on those attributes to others in our circles. What a gift! We also become willing to sacrifice for the Lord because He has given so much to us.

Contentment isn't easy to come by, especially during weeks of conspicuous consumption. However, it is possible—with God's help.

## ARE YOU AT PEACE WITH WHERE GOD HAS PLACED YOU?

*These things I have spoken unto you, that in me ye might have peace. In the world ye shall have tribulation: but be of good cheer; I have overcome the world.*

JOHN 16:33

## WHY IS PEACE SO DIFFICULT?

*And let the peace of God rule in your hearts.*

COLOSSIANS 3:15

## DOES PEACE EQUAL CIRCUMSTANCES
## OR A STATE OF MIND FOR YOU? WHY?

*Mark the perfect man, and behold the upright:*
*for the end of that man is peace.*

PSALM 37:37

## WHAT *IS* PEACEFUL IN YOUR LIFE?
## HOW CAN YOU MAKE THAT YOUR FOCUS?

*Return unto thy rest, O my soul;*
*for the L*ORD *hath dealt bountifully with thee.*

**P**SALM **116:7**

## DESCRIBE A MEMORY OF PEACE AT CHRISTMAS.

*He maketh me to lie down in green pastures:*
*he leadeth me beside the still waters.*

**PSALM 23:2**

# What does peace look like? Sound like? Feel like?

# Peace in Forgiveness

*And hearken thou to the supplication of thy servant, and of thy people Israel, when they shall pray toward this place: and hear thou in heaven thy dwelling place: and when thou hearest, forgive.*

1 KINGS 8:30

During the holidays, we often spend time with people who've hurt us. How do we move on—forgive, let go, and perhaps even find a restored relationship—when our friends or family members have deeply wounded us?

We can't control others' behavior, but we can make changes in our own lives:

1. *Set healthy boundaries.* Leave damaging patterns behind, as much as it depends on you, and establish new patterns. Don't enable bad behavior, and protect yourself. If it's possible, try to establish a relationship based on healthier forms of communication.

2. *Begin again.* Grieve the past, but also determine that you will not dwell there. If you can, find out about your loved one's past in order to understand his or her choices and actions. When we can empathize or have compassion for the wounds others have experienced, it can give us perspective and soften our hearts.

3. *Realize our Heavenly Father is the only perfect person.* Just as we make mistakes, our family members and friends make mistakes too. God, through Jesus, imparted grace to us when we were at our most sinful, and He enables us to give that grace to others. He can give us the understanding, forgiveness, and strength to move forward.

Keep seeking Him and falling on His mercy. Live in the light of His love, and pray for those who have wounded you. Remember that He has forgiven you—and with His help, you can forgive too.

## What steps can you take to bring peace to turbulent relationships?

*Blessed are the peacemakers:*
*for they shall be called the children of God.*

MATTHEW 5:9

# HOW IS BEING A PEACEMAKER ONE OF
# THE GREATEST GIFTS YOU CAN GIVE?

*Peace I leave with you, my peace I give unto you:
not as the world giveth, give I unto you. Let not
your heart be troubled, neither let it be afraid.*

**JOHN 14:27**

# WHAT DOES REAL PEACE MEAN IN YOUR LIFE OR IN THE WORLD?

*For God is not the author of confusion, but of peace.*

1 CORINTHIANS 14:33

## How does focusing on God, who is in control, bring peace when things are out of control?

*Be perfect, be of good comfort, be of one mind, live in peace;*
*and the God of love and peace shall be with you.*

2 CORINTHIANS 13:11

## IN WHAT WAYS CAN YOU AND YOUR FAMILY MAKE PEACE A PRIORITY THIS HOLIDAY?

*And the peace of God, which passeth all understanding,*
*shall keep your hearts and minds through Christ Jesus.*

PHILIPPIANS 4:7

**HOW HAVE YOU SEEN THE HOLY SPIRIT BRING PEACE TO YOUR LIFE?**

*Thou wilt keep him in perfect peace,*
*whose mind is stayed on thee.*

ISAIAH 26:3

# Hope

## The Hope You Long For

✿

*Jesus said unto him, If thou canst believe,*
*all things are possible to him that believeth.*

MARK 9:23

When we look around our sin-sick world, it's difficult to remember that God sent Jesus not only to redeem the world but also to restore it. One day all broken things will be made new. All nations will be at peace; all women, men, and children will bow to the King of kings, and He will reign justly.

For now, we're like the Israelites in the 400 silent years between the last word of God's prophets and the announcement of the birth of Jesus: confused, full of doubt and despair. We feel forgotten. *Is God really coming back?* we wonder. *Are His promises really true?*

They are. One day, the Bible says, Jesus will destroy hunger, devastation, and degradation. He will deal justice to those who have captured and pillaged and tortured; He will give peace to the victims of cruel oppression.

Satan roams the earth for now, but soon, our righteous King will destroy him and all his demons. Humans are victims—for now—of his schemes, but not for long. God will cup our faces in His hands, brush the tears off our cheeks, and kiss our heads as He holds us close.

Our King is coming, just as He came over 2,000 years ago to a virgin who found favor. He is coming in truth and power. Until then, we hold onto God's hands as He holds our hearts. And we share our faith, so that others will find

*And now, Lord, what wait I for? my hope is in thee.*

PSALM 39:7

# WHAT ARE YOUR HOPES FOR THE FUTURE?

# WHAT ARE YOUR HOPES FOR THIS CHRISTMAS?

*Now the God of hope fill you with all joy and peace in believing,*
*that ye may abound in hope, through the power of the Holy Ghost.*

ROMANS 15:13

# Are you more hopeful around the holidays? Why?

*But sanctify the Lord God in your hearts: and be ready always to give an answer to every man that asketh you a reason of the hope that is in you with meekness and fear.*

1 PETER 3:15

# How can you bring hope to a world without hope?

*For whatsoever things were written aforetime were written for our learning, that we through patience and comfort of the scriptures might have hope.*

ROMANS 15:4

**HOW DOES RECALLING THE FIRST CHRISTMAS—**

**AND OTHER SCRIPTURES—GIVE YOU HOPE?**

# Our Hope

*I have waited for thy salvation, O Lord.*

GENESIS 49:18

---

We often want immediate resolutions to our issues. We long for God to press the "fix-it" button and send enough money to erase all our debts. We want physical or emotional healing but don't want to work for it. And when He makes us wait, we falter and begin to lose hope.

Sometimes, the Father cries "Enough!" and answers our desperate pleas for deliverance. For instance, He told Joseph in a dream to leave the place where he and Mary were staying with the baby Jesus. At other times, though, He doles out daily—even minute-by-minute—grace.

Why does God tarry when He could snap His celestial fingers and fix our problems in a second? He's powerful enough, after all.

For one thing, He knows our nature. If He answered all our prayers and we never had a need—physical, emotional, financial—we would get complacent. (Think about the Israelites—God parted the Red Sea and freed them from slavery, and still they rebelled. They doubted and complained. That's why He gave them manna, which would rot if they tried to store it overnight. He wanted them to trust Him for their every breath.)

At all times, friends, *He* is our miracle. God sent Jesus into the world that first Christmas to be our living water and our bread of life. He strengthens our weary hearts and supplies us with living hope. . .second by second, minute by minute, hour by hour, and day by day.

IN WHAT WAYS IS GOD YOUR HOPE EACH AND EVERY MOMENT?

*Therefore my heart is glad, and my glory rejoiceth: my flesh also shall rest in hope.*

PSALM 16:9

# WHAT GIVES YOU HOPE?

*Now faith is the substance of things hoped for,*
*the evidence of things not seen.*

HEBREWS 11:1

# How are hope and faith related?

........................................................................
........................................................................
........................................................................
........................................................................
........................................................................
........................................................................
........................................................................
........................................................................
........................................................................
........................................................................
........................................................................
........................................................................
........................................................................
........................................................................
........................................................................
........................................................................
........................................................................
........................................................................
........................................................................
........................................................................
........................................................................
........................................................................
........................................................................

*For in thee, O LORD, do I hope:*
*thou wilt hear, O Lord my God.*

PSALM 38:15

*In hope of eternal life, which God, that cannot lie, promised before the world began.*

TITUS 1:2

HOW DOES THE HOPE OF HEAVEN CHANGE
YOUR PERSPECTIVE HERE ON EARTH?

*For thou art my hope, O Lord GOD:*
*thou art my trust from my youth.*

PSALM 71:5

# WHAT WERE YOUR CHRISTMAS WISHES AS A CHILD?

# The Hope of Compassion

*Finally, be ye all of one mind, having compassion one of another, love as brethren, be pitiful, be courteous.*

1 PETER 3:8

---

Because of God's gift of Jesus, and the gifts the magi brought to the baby, Christmas is known as a season of giving. But what would it look like if we had the same spirit of charity every day of the year?

Christians are called to this kind of compassion. In the Gospels, Jesus is often described as being moved with *splagchnos* (compassion) toward the lame, sick, and hurting. And ". . .every time Jesus was moved with compassion, it always resulted in a healing, deliverance, resurrection, supernatural provision, or some other action that changed someone's life. You see, compassion always produces action. The force of compassion cannot leave a person in the sad condition in which he was found; it moves one to do something to change that other person's situation."*

What has God delivered you from? How has He provided miraculously for you? The ways God has worked in your life can provide the basis of a ministry to others. Take the compassion God has given to you, and turn it into compassion for others.

Has He redeemed you from drug abuse? Train to work as a substance abuse counselor. Has God freed you from depression? Share your story with others, and give them hope. As you look at your life, you will see threads of resurrection. Ask the Father how He may want to use those threads to weave a tapestry of grace that will give glory to Him for generations to come.

*Renner, Rick, *Sparkling Gems from the Greek* (Tulsa: Teach All Nations/Harrison House, 2003),

**HOW HAS GOD PREPARED YOU TO SHARE HOPE
WITH OTHERS NO MATTER WHAT TIME OF YEAR?**

*Hope deferred maketh the heart sick:*
*but when the desire cometh, it is a tree of life.*

PROVERBS 13:12

*For our sakes, no doubt, this is written: that he that ploweth should plow in hope; and that he that thresheth in hope should be partaker of his hope.*

1 CORINTHIANS 9:10

# WHERE DO YOU SEE HOPE AT WORK IN YOUR CHURCH?

## IN YOUR COMMUNITY?

*For there is hope of a tree, if it be cut down, that it will sprout again, and that the tender branch thereof will not cease.*

JOB 14:7

# WHAT HOPEFUL STORY OF FAITH CAN YOU
# PASS ON TO SOMEONE THIS CHRISTMAS?

And what shall I more say? for the time would fail me to tell of Gedeon, and of Barak, and of Samson, and of Jephthae; of David also, and Samuel, and of the prophets: who through faith subdued kingdoms, wrought righteousness, obtained promises, stopped the mouths of lions.

HEBREWS 11:32–33

## WHO INSPIRES YOU TO HOPE? WHY?

*For the law made nothing perfect, but the bringing in of*
*a better hope did; by the which we draw nigh unto God.*

HEBREWS 7:19

## WHAT ABOUT CHRISTMAS SYMBOLIZES HOPE TO YOU?

# The Hope of Blessing

*And in thy seed shall all the nations of the earth be blessed;*
*because thou hast obeyed my voice.*

GENESIS 22:18

---

One of the things we hear about at Christmastime is *regifting*. The word means to give someone something you've been given. . .such as a sweater you don't like. Workplaces and Bible study groups have "White Elephant" or "Tacky Christmas" parties where each person brings a dud of a gift. The group plays a game where participants can steal a gift they like—or one they find especially hideous and hilarious—once or twice. It's all in good fun, until you receive Aunt Matilda's moldy fruitcake.

However, what if we as believers turned the concept upside down and saw regifting as a Gospel-sharing opportunity?

God has given us His Son, salvation, and eternal life. He has given us spiritual gifts, the Holy Spirit, and His presence. Why not regift those things to a world in need? When we use the things God has given us to bless others, we serve and magnify Him. We often talk about God's blessings in our lives, but did you know that we can bless the Lord?

Wow.

What gifts can you regift this year? Perhaps your father-in-law needs the same gentle patience God has shown with you. Maybe your coworker is desperate for a listening ear and loving, wise counsel, which the Father has provided you countless times. Give those gifts away, freely and graciously. In doing so, you'll be putting a smile on your Creator's face and spreading the Good News of Jesus.

What a holy privilege we've been given!

*Wherefore comfort yourselves together,
and edify one another, even as also ye do.*

1 Thessalonians 5:11

# WHO NEEDS A DOSE OF HOPE THIS HOLIDAY SEASON?

*But if we hope for that we see not,*
*then do we with patience wait for it.*

ROMANS 8:25

# WHY SHOULD WE NEVER LOSE HOPE?

*But I will hope continually, and will*
*yet praise thee more and more.*

Psalm 71:14

*Be of good courage, and he shall strengthen your heart,*
*all ye that hope in the LORD.*

PSALM 31:24

*Almighty King, thank You for coming as a baby to redeem the world from sin. Thank You for Your forgiveness and mercy. Forgive me for the times I am too busy to meditate on Your goodness. Forgive me for the moments I haven't spent worshipping and listening. Quiet my heart, Jesus. Speak Your truth to me. I want to know You better and make You known to those who desperately need Your saving grace. During this busy season, help me to find—and create—spaces of time to sit with You. I love You, precious Lord. Amen.*